The Days After

Rebecca Parfitt

Listen Softly London
333 Muswell Hill Broadway
London
N10 1BY

ListenSoftlyLondon.com
@ListenSoftlyLDN

THE DAYS AFTER
COPYRIGHT © 2017 by Rebecca Parfitt

First Edition, April 2017

Cover Design by Aaron Lipschitz
Edited by Dominic Stevenson
Typeset by Aaron Lipschitz

ISBN: 978-0-9935353-4-5

Published in the United Kingdom

The Days After

For Camilla

Rebecca Parfitt

Reader,
the heart will heal
and when it does
make a flower of the scar

The Days After

Contents

The Tattooist's Wife   8

THE DAYS BEFORE

Snapped-Bone Branch   10
At the River   11
The Presence   12
Knowing   14
The Bay   15
Spaghetti   16
The Journey to End   17
Dialogue in a dark place   18
After the Tate Modern   19
Exit at the Barbican   20
Sea Bed   21
Love in the Crackling Deep   22
Stitches   23
The Wedding Gift   24
The Un-wanting   25
Sleepwalking   26
Mealtime   27
We Pretend   28
Song of after   30
To the children we never had   31
Spring Equinox   32

Rebecca Parfitt

Undressed   33
Nostalgia   34

THE DAYS

'Precious Fragments'   36
Arsonist of Hearts   40
The Island   41
Bullets on the Path   42
Moth   43
Path   44
Night Carriage   45
Birds   46
Visitation   47
House   48
Mother Daughter Hamam   50
Courtyard at West 5   52
Sister   53
Something Resembling Homesickness   54

THE DAYS AFTER

Tram-ride, Berlin, Feb 2015   56

How to Wear a Suitcase   57

Changing Room   58

Piercing Heart   60

I have a wandering heart   61

Honeymoon Period   62

A woman's life is like the rosary, up and down, 63

All of the things that led me to you   64

Seed   66

Spoon   67

Rebecca Parfitt

The Tattooist's Wife

Draw on me. My skin
is parchment for you.

Gather your land together.
I am an island
for the swallow on your forearm.

I am a desert,
waiting for your breath to blow the clouds,
across my cheeks, to ruffle the leaves against my chest.

Draw a lion over my heart and I will feel it flex its paws,
dig for blood.
And the wild woman – Eve of my body –
will ride him through my branches.

You will slide ink underneath and wrap me in birds
dipped in red, blue, green
and the flowers will bloom, always,
when you touch me.

Cover me, so you must search every part
to kiss me inside.
Set your arms around me,
let the swallow cross the wide gasp of air between us.

The Days Before

Rebecca Parfitt

Snapped-Bone Branch

I brought home a stick of poisonous berries.
A lightning branch ripped from a tree,
torn white flesh under bark,
remembered, you almost ruined me.

The berries hold their own bulbs of blood
my capsuled love – a flesh wound in my little fisted hand;
burst heart, snapped-bone branch,
sprawling fingers reach
as you claw your way into my dreams.

I pick the globules, put the berries into my mouth
and try to murder my nights full of you.
An owl's call empties into the folds of darkness,
senses a predator's hunger just like his.

If I could send you from my body with a long cry
I'd have you disappeared to the biting air.
Yet this lightning branch spreads across the sky,
my forked fingers dig in,
these poisonous droplets seek you out.

At the River

I dreamt about you again last night.
The river,
flowers. Togetherness.

My long yellow dress blowing in the wind,
our arms wrapped around each other
as we walked the path
through the garden
to the boat.

But this time we did not speak.
I was silent,
you waited for me to say it.

The words always at the edge of my tongue,
like barbs.
To say them would draw blood,
would reveal us in our truth.

The river only knows
my tongue remained still
and you turned your back
and walked away.

Rebecca Parfitt

The Presence

The bell out to sea rang steadily,
rain pounded against the windows.

Our bed taking a beating of another kind.
But I had something else on my mind,

a sense of things wrapping themselves up,
putting ourselves away, coming to the end of the world
and seeing nothing at the edge.

Our expensive sea view blurred by raindrops and wind,
a glimpse of the future.
The presence was there, roaming the beach
at the back of my mind.
From our hotel window, I watched the palm-trees
flatten sideways,
the plastic chairs move across the patio in the wind.

I was at sea gathering my thoughts into a net
and you cupped my breasts, held me like a trophy,
splitting me, you found the anemone
and we cast out again,
rocking fervently.
You were the only one to find Aphrodite's shells:
pink fingernails – all pearl.

At dinner, over a cracked lobster claw and candlelight,
you gave me the reason you loved me.
I took that reason away,
swallowed it down.

The wind never stopped battering at the windows,
the pub signs swung like flags in the streets
and doors flung open, though no-one entered.
A gale blew inside my head
but it was your fingers that ruffled my hair.

How could you have known
there was something else with us
on the beach that day?
When I stood under the arch of the rock, calling you,
as your image was swept out.
You disappeared into the long smile of the shore,
and the waves turned over and over,
showing me nothing of my loss.

Rebecca Parfitt

Knowing

My back hurts, I say,
drawing in my breath as you get closer.
I lean with palms flat against the wall,
hands outspread,
taking the weight.

Your knuckles knead further,
up my spine
follow the notches,
closer,
your hands open, smooth me out,
then a tremble, lips parting,
my skin swallows a kiss.

The pain is gone. Miraculous.
Dissolved to nothing.

You say you have always wanted me.

I turn and face you as though this is normal
and the silence of relief lingers in the air:
a cloud waiting to be dispersed by the wind.

The Bay

The merry-go-round played out with grim enthusiasm
as we passed by,
the skirt of our black umbrella angled
against the wind.
We were the only people walking the promenade
of empty chain restaurants
devoid of charm.
Latin music piped out through crummy speakers,
a delusion of a summer holiday somewhere hot,
somewhere else,
somewhere not here.
Yet the chairs stacked up against the walls dripped
with rain
and we huddled together to keep warm.

I bought you chips to eat in the salted sea air,
vinegared with a sharp gull's cry,
and from the jetty we watched tourists venture out
onto the platform,
take a photo, clouded by the dark sky,
and scuttle away like insects,
enduring little of the chilly British weather.
In the distance the merry-go-round played
but still did not turn.

That night we drank the world
and rolled heavily into bed,
murmured of making babies between things unsaid.

　　　　Rebecca Parfitt

Spaghetti

Over spaghetti I am reminded of you –
perhaps it's this mess that makes me think of
looking at the view whilst pissing in a sand dune,
into the darkness, into the wind, into the long grass;
watching the sporadic flashing lights of boats
and oil tankers
docked offshore for the night;
of the sea below, shushing us, shushing us.
Where you made a fire for your lady
in the dirt sand
and we played 'house'
and fucked whilst the horizon winked and blinked
all night
until it was over
as quickly as my sand dune tinkle,
a beautiful necessity,
a beautiful view
of the road in the distance
where nothing approached
and nothing left.

But over a plate of spaghetti
I go back to that place
and my ghosted memory haunts awhile.
Perhaps we are still there, together,
there's just no way back,
the distance rubbed us out.

The Journey to End

You slept, napping in the afternoon,
a sprig of honeysuckle by the bedside.
I stood naked by the window,
curtains blowing, coffee boiling on the hob,
watching the French buzz around
on scooters in the square.
I was nothing but soft fruit, ready to expire,
and you left me like a bruised apple.

Here, I silently declared,
I would go anywhere with you.

In the second hand shop I picked out combs:
electric green, tortoiseshell,
running my thumbnail across the prongs.
I let the cherry cognac chocolate burst in my mouth,
the red wine spill,
the bath overflow
and your chaos tie me in knots.

On the last night a thunderstorm broke
as my fingers wandered the tangles of your hair.
Waiting. Waiting.
But you never dirtied your tongue with the cries of
I love you.
Love was a word too big to fit in your mouth.

Rebecca Parfitt

Dialogue in a dark place

The leaves are turning, you said.
And I shook and shook and shook myself from you
'til my body was a bare trunk.

Then you gathered my discard,
made a pyre and watched
as my hair caught fire and I burned sweet smoke –
the scent of our darkness,
our deep descent from the open sky.

After the Tate Modern

Out into the wet smear of the Southbank
under heavy dirty rain, we paused to kiss.
Then scatter like birds from our embrace
to run into the sheltered avenue of trees
shining blue and white
with lights
we ran underneath the bridge
through rising puddles
past the busker who was singing our song
the huddled skaters
and the homeless –   but too late.
Our chests heaving and cheeks red
the train left us behind on the platform
winking and flashing electric sparks
out into the smudged darkness of Saturday night air.

Rebecca Parfitt

Exit at the Barbican

Your words echo through my mind,
sharp Kandinsky lines jabbing,
itching inside.
It is uncomfortable to know this detail of pain
sears through you and I can do nothing to help
but find fleeting distraction in art
displayed inside neat glass cases.
While at home, he packs boxes,
removing fragments of his life,
his museum of self,
his museum of you,
and these are the pieces,
this is the gift shop to remember you by.

Sea Bed

You want to hold onto me,
fearful I might drown if you let go.
Our sea bed, white waved sheets
showed a rough crossing
to a place neither of us knew yet.

You cling to me as I try to get out
to reach the sunlit floor of morning
to see what the surface is like without you.
With each movement I tip the sea bed a little more
and the white waved sheets rise higher
and the salt water from our bodies seeps in.
I *might* drown if you let go.

Can I hold you? You ask.
Only if you let go, I reply.

Rebecca Parfitt

Love in the Crackling Deep

"The beauty of your arm is exactly like that of your body,
if I didn't know your body I would want it,
just from seeing the shape of your arm" – Anaïs Nin

The air between us is leaden.
You clumsily reach in,
pulling threads around me,
the strands of hair from my face.
Holding the parts you feel safe with,
the parts that won't lead you anywhere else,
won't lead you into another silence
more difficult than this.

When we held hands, like children,
we didn't know what to do next
but reaffirm *this*. This empty space
that could have been us,
that is not yet filled,
is an imprint of us,
without *us*.

So I held the skin between your finger and thumb
until you withdrew, said nothing
and watched me leave,
entering a gale that threw your fingerprints
across my body, marking me
all over again.

Stitches

I'm unpicking the stitches you sewed
as I lay under you, your fingers fine as needles
fraying my skin, threading yourself inside.

I find pieces of you I'd forgotten I carried,
pieces I can't remove.
I want to turn myself inside out and slowly,
unwind the thread, let the trail fall behind me
as you follow

       but I'll be gone when you turn the corner,
      just a snag of my dress caught on a bramble
    and the blood of berries left crushed on the road,
      replacing the heart you once held in your hands.

Rebecca Parfitt

The Wedding Gift

The date sits in my diary like a tombstone,
I construct myself around it,
dressing up a smile.
What can I bring that you don't already have?

But myself when you wanted me forever
on a single day.

The day I unfolded like a rose at dawn,
as though it was my first feeling of sun,
my first look at the daylight shape
and you wore your surprise underneath,
in the shade where I could not see you uncoil away,
suddenly darkened behind a cloud
of the unforgiven things you passed my way.

I wear the gift of infidelity on my body –
a mark of thorns from the rose between.

Now my wedding gift lies unopened
and you forget the day you gave me away.

The Un-wanting

The lies fringed by your lashes,
hide the essence of you –
the piece I was looking for
and couldn't find.
I saw my reflection –
sitting there,
in the gloomy green room
waiting for you.
Willing to strip my tongue of its taste for you,
and the words which slipped up from the deep
that emptied out so readily
to be met with nothing.
They disappeared into the wind
in this place where I called out for you, once,
and you killed me with silence.

Now I wait for the moment
when I am the smoking gun,

emptied of you.

Rebecca Parfitt

Sleepwalking

I return to you each time,
each time, a little further,
edging closer in,
returning to the beach
as the sea breathes long and hard,
pounding up and down the pebbles.

This was where you split me in half,
pitted the core,
then discarded it like a stone,
never looking back
to see the ripples in the water
spread their rings around you.

Mealtime

There's an autumn light
that shifts into a crisp dusk.
I eat a meal of orange chicken and rice,
corn on the cob – the world beginning to blaze
and fray at winter approaching.
I am the only person at this table
and I think of you
sitting in that chair opposite,
tucking into this meal that would have surprised you:
it tastes good. The rice is just right
for a change,
I made it just right.

But I eat in silence,
hollow out the room
as I take each bite.

Rebecca Parfitt

We Pretend

Nothing
happened here.
Everything
looks as it should.
We sit,
like we could
hold each other forever
in this room holding
ourselves together.
Everything placed
ordinarily,
arbitrarily
without care,
scattered belongings
no longer matter
like they did.
It seems impossible
to separate,
so we coast inside
these silent walls,
sleeping without waking.
Each day I recognise you
less as the wholeness of me:
my complete, good side.
The one I live for less and less.
I forget that anything
was once possible for us.
I long to wake up

to a time before yesterday
but this is my waking world
where your light,
like the sun, lowers
then disappears.

Rebecca Parfitt

Song of after

She's there, in the corner of the room,
the thing you played to make me come.
Our first conversation held over her
to our last,
in song, in breath and manual dexterity
tighten, then release her strings to hear my chords.
Her body was my body – though, she is more curvaceous,
darker skinned, exotic, a hollowed stomach
unlike mine.
Then why, if you love her, did you leave her behind?
To remind me of how we used to sing together,
over my body, hers and yours?
Her waist fits yours and your fingers caress her neck
though she does not bend towards you, or away
like I do.
But she and I sit together, alone,
unable to play each other,
silent, opposite, detached.
We cannot play without your fingers on us,
we do not sing without you here.

To the children we never had

It's not that we couldn't have created you.
Creation was never something we had a problem with.
You were already out there, somewhere,
to have been born to us or any other
would have made no difference to you.
It was a happening that did not happen.
It was the darkness that let you go unnoticed,
you were unfound, and we never really asked for you.
Instead, invented names, faces,
you were the undeveloped thought
deep in our subconscious
and nothing makes nothing happen.
So eternally the never in our ending.

Rebecca Parfitt

Spring Equinox

The day before your birthday
I shed my clothes, piece by piece.
It means nothing to have them on,
they are not who I am.
Silk between my palms
hangs in the air between us –
the gap that swallowed us
whole.

The dress you liked hangs, untouched,
in-between the pieces you have not seen.
These belong somewhere else now,
on someone else's body.
The zip – a mouth cracked open,
I step out of your *beholden*,
drop my clothes into the bag,
feel the pull of empty sleeves:
a beckon into glancing back.

So here I am, another year gone,
counting the rings around my finger
with my trunk of past selves:
a body in pieces for someone else to own.

Undressed

I still haven't washed my dress since that day.
It lies in the bottom of the basket with wine stains,
and half-arsed, low-class sex
all over it.

I won't touch it now,
I've nothing but the dirt to remind me
of your fingers unbuttoning,
peeling me out with eyes of delight,
slipping it off like a sweetie wrapper
discarding it to the floor –
as though you really thought it were possible to eat me
as no one had ever done before.

Rebecca Parfitt

Nostalgia

I circle around the places we have been together,
as if stepping inside would break the floor beneath.
Edging the memory, herding it out of my mind,
it wanders reluctantly past that place
where we kissed.
My other self would have you slip inside –
and I am hardly sure if it did not happen
but this pathway runs unseen into the distance.

I remember a passer-by glance aside,
our embrace meant nothing to him,
he did not know what I held
and I held you knowing
I will never hold that much wanting again.
And all the places we have ever been together
float like bubbles, ever un-bursting.
The perfect moment that never was
and never will be again.

THE DAYS

Rebecca Parfitt

'Precious Fragments'

1.

You will know that the letter was the perfect ending and nothing more could have been said. (And the brass hand was the only thing I kept.)

2.

The brass hand formed the shape of our sex against the wall. Made a hole there. Showed me you were once real.

3.

I am fearful of the side of the bed in which you slept. As if you are still there. Until I wash you from my sheets.

4.

Something of a curse crawled in and stayed for a couple of years. Nothing was safe.

5.

Afterwards, my mind filled with the buzzing blur of enormous reality. Time stretched so far away that each hour had me locked up.

What purpose in the aftermath when I am left with nothing but myself?

6.

I tried to tidy any trace of you away each time you came over.

I should have tidied more.

7.

When I reached for the sugar bowl I could see time marked by you: a perfectly round crevice in the white mound, the hole of your digging.

8.

I remember how you smelled, watching the tide come in, the fuzz of sweat, cigarettes and salt. You loved to see the tide come in.

Things approaching are easier to watch.

9.

From you I learned that people are signifiers, symbolic sometimes.

Rebecca Parfitt

10.

I watched the ducklings on the lake treading lily-pads
whilst you told me why you didn't want children.
They had only just been born.

You are the architect of your world, how can I
shape you?

11.

Our conversation was this: 'Philosophy hangs in the
clouds above.'

'You should know one thing cannot exist without
the other –'

12.

       'Predestined'
       'Predetermined'
       'It's not all just arbitrary.'
       'It can't be arbitrary.'
       'It's divine.'

13.

Something intervenes when it has to, but only when
it has to.

14.

Something intervened.

15.

One day I will have a door of my own, in a house
of my own and I will fasten the brass hand to it and
I will hear it knock and I will think of you as the
sound echoes through the house. I will suddenly
be back here, where I am now, for a second. And
before I open it, for just a moment I will forget that
it will not be you standing there on the doorstep but
someone else instead.

16.

'I know that the expectation will go with time.
With time we are freed from the habits of ourselves
circling each other.'

Rebecca Parfitt

Arsonist of Hearts

I made a fire out of you,
on the concrete floor below my window,
where I watched your flowers die.
I gathered two cards and a dried autumn leaf,
kept to remind me of a time
that no longer mattered.
Struck my fury into flame
the flame died to ash
and the ash blew away.

I lit a cigarette, smoked it to the end
and flicked it away.
That butt was you – a short-lived nothing
that did its best to choke me.

The Island

We waited for the tide to go out
so we could cross to the other side,
reach the island.

But we waited and waited
and the tide held out, against us.

My face – moon still above the rock pools –
looked down.
They showed me the death of things:
shells frail and empty, stones worn,
lifeless in the salt stiff water.

Even the gulls held back, they felt my longing
for another day,
for this time to pass quickly.

And still the tide, no lower,
just a rushing torrent of froth on the rocks
and the wind buffeted us with the tension in the air
until the rain started,
dripped banal circles into the pools
and we, waiting for the tide to part our way through.

Though somewhere it lost its course
and we could only look on
at the island, in its strength and loneliness.

　　　　　　　　Rebecca Parfitt

Bullets on the Path

That day on the path of burnt gorse
I could hear the crackle of things being let go,
the last segment of *this* –
I heard the words coming in the sea breeze:
nothing lasts.

And there it was, at the edges,
waiting for me to notice the shape
of things to come.
Nothing *happened*, just words unravelling the past,
letting go like bullets from a gun.
Now it's all changed.

To test impermanence,
I drew a shape in the sand,
then watched the waves take it away.

Moth

Shadows on the wall
stretch towards something I can't see.
A moth passes through the open window,
its movement quick, aimless, blurred body of chaos
tumbling into darkness.
Propelled towards something it sees
but cannot push through,
it bats against the bulb over and over again,
singeing wings, shedding dust,
its movement growing heavier and heavier.
The spin of energy suddenly lost,
it folds itself against the wall,
remains still, like a blackened fingernail,
wounded.

Rebecca Parfitt

Path

In my hazy sleep I reached out for you and caught
sight of myself in the mirror. Something was
different. My hair was much longer, as though it
had grown overnight. I could not recall the last time
I looked at myself. I had the tell-tale marks on my
skin, he's been here, I thought, but it's all over now.

I can remember watching for the handle to turn, for
the shadows flitting about under the door – to know
I am no longer alone. I waited for the ticking of a
faceless clock, for movement in the trees, to see the
paths of things leaving.

No time but shadows against the wall – shortening,
lengthening. I go nowhere in it. Just my hair growing
as time passes. A door slams. I wait for the handle
to turn, for this aching pendulum to pass.

Night Carriage

An infinity of shadows spread outwards –
a strange puppetry in the hands of trees.
Through the window plays a theatre,
nothing but the reflection of my face,
ghostly, blurred,
and the backs of seats rising up
like tombstones.
Darkness suddenly punctuated by street lights,
on and on into the distance.

The words on the page of the book in my lap
float there, mirrored in the glass.
I see threads of light
and the train tracks shining on the wet ground
waiting, like snakes in the rain.

Rebecca Parfitt

Birds

From your bedside I watched wrens stuff their fat
bodies into the hedgerow outside,
eating a feast at your expense.

The birds were at your shoulders, pulling worms
from your ears,
chattering.
They made a tree of your body,
made a nest of your wild red heath.

Time ate itself, became oversized,
the clocks swollen fat:
hours filled hours.
Only you could reset them.
And the birds about your shoulders would not leave
you alone.
I plucked their feathers from your pillow –
unnecessary needles pricking at the surface,
until my father's dream was woken by a nightmare:
A click of the front door and your figure, shoeless, tiny,
already halfway down the street – in the frost,
chasing birds into the darkness.

I willed them to drop from the sky,
to wrestle you free from *that* I could not see.

Visitation

I have met you twice to reconcile.
I see the familiarity of your torso,
I could still describe you now.
Intimacy polarises the memory.

On one of the days I thought I was going to die,
a lady in the street stopped me to ask
if I wanted my fortune told,
to see my future.
'I've already seen it,' I replied.

Not so strange then
when that night you returned to my bed
and told me of your suffering.
I wonder, do I visit you too?

These visitations have become more frequent since.
I ask,
'when will this unfinished business of longing cease?'

Rebecca Parfitt

House

'In making for ourselves a place to live,
we first spread a parasol to throw a shadow on the earth,
and in the pale light of the shadow we put together a house.'

Jun' Ichiko Tanizaki

Underneath the bough of sleep
I waited for the walls to build around me:
a canopy above, silk stretched across
this, my shelter, my place where the shadows fall.
I imagined our home and took it with me,
folding the edges with my fingers,
smoothing the walls with my hands.

My eyes carry the view – even now,
through the window I see
the runner-beans, the rhubarb growing slowly outside,
working their way towards the sunlight.
They build their own canopy,
their flowers like offspring –
babies in blankets.
At night the moon shines,
silver disc encircled by the black deep.
There I am, underneath,
clutching hold of my childhood,
the porcelain lion and the musical box,
watching the ballerina turning,
fast at first, then slowly the tune
drags and stretches to nothing,

as if the sound is squeezed out
until it loses breath and stops.
The ballerina is left staring into the mirror,
and I at the ballerina.
I close the lid letting the shadow darken the past,
then slide underneath the bough of sleep
and wait for the walls to build around me.

I imagined our home and took it with me,
folding the edges with my fingers,
smoothing the walls with my hands.
Here I built you a house when the snow cleared.
I built you a house when the first crocus appeared.
Come under me,
under the shelter of the bowed tree.

Rebecca Parfitt

Mother Daughter Hamam

We sat at the edge of my grandfather's bed
his breathing shallowed
as though his lungs were disappearing –
his soul extracted by breath.
My father held his hand, felt him lift from the bed.

'Look to the ceiling, wave, say goodbye, up there,
in the corners – that's where he is.'
You said.

Two days later we emerged from the January murk,
into an amber scented, prune sweet place,
surrounded by the snow-topped Atlas Mountains,
we reeled at the cold African rain,
wandering into the unknown,
dodging from scooters, buses, horses
and donkeys.
Into the square, the call to prayer
interjected with the cries of 'parapluie'.

Our shelter was the dripping souks.
Sweet fresh mint tea steamed
in silver pots as we passed shop after shop
each were an entrance to Aladdin's cave
offering better than the last
until we were lost in something labyrinthine.

On the last day we lay, almost naked,
in the dark womb of the steam room.
I watched as the girl rubbed your body clean,
comparing your shape with mine.
Contours observed, I saw the truth of family,
in likeness and in difference:
coffee dark nipples to rose petal light.
I thought of my grandfather who had four,
wondered if that was true,
or just another familial myth.

Your dead skin washed away,
it was my turn,
the girl took my hand
and with her touch I felt my skin unpeeling,
falling away,
like a chrysalis I shed my cocoon
to be released – a butterfly – into the air.

Rebecca Parfitt

Courtyard at West 5

The decaying limb of 'West 5' marks the end,
impending.
An absence of care perhaps,
or a mirror to the mind of all of us
who stand on the border looking out
or in.

The courtyard seems abandoned,
but notice the plants:
left in the hands of chaos
the most neglected share a moment of clarity
once in a while
natural order emerges –
something wants to grow.

The plants are perfect – full of wellness,
they are doing what they were meant to,
they lack control, that's all.
There is nothing here to tame them,
only winter.
And even the darkest December day still has light
and spring will always begin again
to get the plants stirring.

Sister

She touches my arm,
reaching out
from the edge of sleep,
gently clasps it,
checking I'm still there
before sliding back
to her sequence of dreams.

I wake as a line of wintry light
squeezes through the curtain,
forgetting she's not there
but asleep in another town.

The early morning shadows
mark the space of absence
and a crease in the sheets
folds over an imprint of her body,
left behind.

Rebecca Parfitt

Something Resembling Homesickness

I felt the flutter of a wing, a butterfly
inside my chest, the nauseating pang
of an early memory,
something recognised that sits within.
The butterfly shifts,
rubbing its wing against my ribcage,
releasing a sickness-tugged, dust-rubbed melancholy
until it comes to rest,
positioned always at the centre of my body –
a flesh-flower.
Unable to live outside its warmth,
the butterfly, a sensation realised,
hidden away inside me, shifting, shifting,
resurrected by my mind's
desire to be somewhere else.

THE DAYS AFTER

Rebecca Parfitt

Tram-ride, Berlin, Feb 2015

The unknowable circumstances of the stranger on
the tram: you know nothing of what it took for
them to be there at that time on that seat in that
place. Only that you are both there, both present –
momentarily in the vacuum of time. And if one of
you were to drop a coin, and the other were to pick it
up, at what moment would your collision start?
If. If. If…

I imagine the coin spinning to a halt. Heads he picks
it up, tails he doesn't. But we will never know, since
now is his stop – the door opens into a chill wind.
I watch him disappear into the entrance of the
U-Bahn. The automated voice reassures me:

I am still on my way to where I think I am going.

How to Wear a Suitcase

Empty it first – it is impossible to carry the remnants
of your previous life.

Put the least important things inside –
so it doesn't matter if you lose it on the platform.

Remember: the suitcase will lose you if it wants to.
(And don't put loss in the suitcase,
you don't want to carry that with you.)

Instead, fill it with hope and belongings that belong
elsewhere,
belongings that do not long to belong.
Hold the handle with a straight arm, walk elegantly.
It is not you dragging you at your worst
through the streets.
Do not value its worth.
Do not allow others to value its worth.
Silk lining or not, the items in this compartment
will
be
exchanged.

Rebecca Parfitt

Changing Room

At the photo-automat, I exchanged 24 selves
for 24 frames.
It started with a beret, then sunglasses,
then I thought, *what-the-hell*, and started shedding.
At the Saigon Street cafe
I sat on someone else's table
and peeled the skin off a summer roll.
Inside an abandoned margarine factory in Kreuzberg
I pondered the face of a Geisha I had spray-painted
onto a whitewashed wall –
left a thumbprint in the paint.
A thumbprint was all I had with me.
In the cinema cafe I spotted myself
in the bottom of a bowl of coffee
topped with froth and soggy biscuit crumbs.
I left lipstick on the rim.
Outside a cafe in Potsdamer Platz
I tried to take a selfie, but self was out of view.
I was a perfect blue sky instead.
At the Chameleon theatre I dined alone by candlelight.
My dress turned green.
I wondered if anybody noticed.
Inside Otto Weidt's workshop for the blind
I contemplated the hidden windowless room,
the doorway to which was a wardrobe.
As if the blind don't need to see.
At the film museum I lost my reflection inside
Marlene Dietrich's vanity case –

it was her face I saw –
those half open eyes were not mine.
Infinite selves reflected into the distance.
In the Chinese dumpling restaurant I waited
for my dumpling to cool,
while the dumpling was cooling
I was a blonde woman with two perfect daughters,
sipping champagne.

I think, the more alone I am,
the more invisible I will become.

Later, I remove my clothes for a Berliner
who tells me that 33 is the perfect age.

Later, I remove my clothes for a Brazilian
who refers to his erection as his 'candle'.
He photographs me as a torso, tells me I am beautiful.
Life is easier when you are headless
and puppets are good with no strings attached.

When I go I offer my handkerchief to a stranger in
my train carriage.
I grip my suitcase. It is my changing room.
My life depends on it.

Rebecca Parfitt

Piercing Heart

Last night I shook my feathers
so they would slide through the air
and start a fire with you.

Hawked, I arched my bow,
fingers plucked, I closed one eye,
focussed
                        And missed.

This one was heading outwards,
into blue chaos and dust.
It landed in afterwards
and *before*, you and I,
so there was no record of anything.
Tumbling into the unknown
of the *someone out there* –
not you, not him
but the one who let me down so gently
I never even knew his name.

I have a wandering heart

Hippocrates would have me think it was my womb.
But my heart, it is my heart that won't stay still.

My heart slides from him to you
And back again

Once I thought it was lost,
I woke with the sensation that it was not there.
I felt nothing.
My heart had dug itself from my chest.

My heart slides from you to him
And back again.

My heart murmurs, whispers often.
It bleeds the thought of him,
sinks through my body like a plunging diver
seeking to lie beside him.
I follow the red swill like a shark.
I want it back.

My heart slides from him to you
And back again.

And sometimes when I speak of him, I taste blood.
I am in pain, my heart says,
and wanders to my stomach
where I cannot eat until
I have the heart I want.

Rebecca Parfitt

Honeymoon Period

Those days at first we lie in bed
and the hours move around us
as though we are the centre of a sundial
and these hours are so long
we stretch our bodies from day into night
and sleep is our travelling to tomorrow's possibility

For in this space it is not possible to reset clocks
we may only count our hours as precious eggs
gather them as our bodies slowly turn
into the gnarled roots of trees

A woman's life is like the rosary, up and down,

says the woman who bore six children.

She tells me of her fertility,
her body like the fruit trees
her husband used to tend.
She tells me, you, her grandson,
must give me a child,
she prays you will.
But I know nothing of how to raise children
only that I want to make love for the sake of it
in the sugar plantation
until the need for prayer is as urgent
as a gathering wind.

As we sit on the veranda
I wonder how many rosary beads
have been pushed
and turned by those fingers
that touched you into being.
I need a reason for ritual, or nothing is important.

I feel this aching responsibility, as woman, to bring life.
Yet the hardest thing to carry into being is a child,
raised from the ground, a harvest nurtured
till the flesh ripens.
And the click of the rosary beads still go up
and down.

Rebecca Parfitt

All of the things that led me to you

When there was nothing else left
I turned to the rope.
I gathered it between my feet,
hauled myself up with my arms
but went nowhere.
So I returned to it at the same time
each week.
And each time I got a little further
from the heaviness of the ground.
I became lighter. Shaped by my strength,
the air made a sculpture of me –
though I was inelegant, graceless.
Sometimes I fought, and in revenge,
the rope tore my skin,
bit me, rubbed me, caught me, constricted me
and breathing was something I had to remember.
They told me not to forget to breathe.

Sometimes I won a battle while hanging upside down,
sometimes I dangled by an ankle,
helplessly waiting to be freed.
I feared for my life more than usual.
I let go at times I thought I never would –
against my instinct to clutch, to fold,
to simply hold on, to let go and not shut my eyes,
they told me to, *look where you are going.*
Though this lack of sight gave me courage.
Not seeing what I feared made the journey easier
and when I opened my eyes and looked down,
I saw you there, in a once empty space,
with your hope budding into a twisted rope
of our children's names.

Rebecca Parfitt

Seed

There is a date I can't forget at the back of my mind.
I imagine this: the seed cracking open,
taking root on my hillside –
the wash down to the saltwater opening,
the kernel between.
This is the only way to make love with sour milk,
sour milk and sugar.
And hope the seed is not uprooted,
uprooted, moon dripped
and washed away.

Spoon

Nestled in behind me
you rub my abdomen
searching for the shape of my belly
checking there's room
for one day it will be full
with your baby sleeping
in the dome of our spoon

Rebecca Parfitt

Acknowledgements

Thanks to my editor, Dominic Stevenson, for doing such a wonderful job getting this manuscript into shape and for his thoughtful and insightful input. Thanks to the following publications with whom some of these poems previously appeared: *Dagda*, The Terry Hetherington Award Anthology: *Cheval, The Boston Poetry Magazine, the Cinnamon Press awards anthology: Journey Planner, Behind Many Doors, Silver Apples magazine, Poetry Wales, The Aesthetica creative writing award anthology, 2016*. Thanks to my family whose love, support and encouragement brought me here. To my friends for sharing wisdom, wine and counsel – in particular, Carrie Clark and Natasha Pater. And finally to Gerald, who came along just when he was supposed to – It's true, all good things start with coffee.

69   Rebecca Parfitt

Lightning Source UK Ltd.
Milton Keynes UK
UKOW03f0324240417
299755UK00002B/3/P